HER Rules

A WOMAN'S GUIDE TO WINNING IN LIFE & BUSINESS

A WOMAN'S GUIDE TO WINNING IN LIFE & BUSINESS

Her Rules. ©2016 LaTasha Nicole

All rights reserved. No part of this publication may be reproduced, distributed, or transmitted in any form or by any means, including photocopying, recording, or other electronic or mechanical methods, without the prior written permission of the publisher, except in the case of brief quotations embodied in critical reviews and certain other noncommercial uses permitted by copyright law. Published by The Pivot Point Publishing. First Edition.

ISBN-13: 978-0692690086

Edited by: Barbara Everett
Cover design by: JMH Creative

Dedication

This book is dedicated to all the women out there doing their best. It is my wish that you achieve everything that your heart desires. Remember, it is not over until the clock stops.

To Ariel and Mahogany, the beats of my heart, I thank God that I was entrusted to raise you two beautiful young women. For that I am blessed. Never give up on your dreams.

To my mom, it is because of you that I am me. I thank you for loving me. I appreciate your unconditional love.

Thank you to my 'besties' who keep my ass from jumping off of the nearest bridge. I hope that I haven't driven you all totally nuts.

A dedication to my angel in heaven: Mrs. Elizabeth Jordan.

It can all be so simple, but we'd rather make it hard.

- Lauryn Hill

Dear Self,

I address this letter to myself because I am you, and you are me. If you are reading this, you are most likely in a place of discontent. You are feeling stuck, and you are looking for answers. You want a way out. Right now, you are probably feeling overwhelmed with life and under impressed with some of the things that are happening around you. Many days you wonder, "How the heck did I get here?" You have tried to pull yourself out of the slump, only to slowly slip back down. Am I in your window yet? I told you - I am you and you are me. Women universally struggle with the same types of issues. We battle daily to look good and tackle life while, often times, we feel like shit! (Oh, by the way, I curse. So I apologize in advance if I offend you). It's hard being a girl, and even harder being superwoman.

Women are emotional creatures, and emotions often complicate things that can be so simple.

We wonder, "Does he really like me, or does he have an agenda?"

"Am I good enough?"

"Am I smart enough?"

"Did I do this right?"

"Are my kids at the right school?"
"Is this outfit good enough?"
"What if I dye my hair? Is that too dramatic for my job?"
"Can I actually win this race?"
We have been conditioned to shrink down and play the role of supporter for so long that we have become less than what we can be. As women, we carry baggage that, oftentimes, we aren't even aware of. We subconsciously bring so much from the past with us that we don't even understand why we are unable to focus.

You are brilliant! You know what you want, and you know how to get there. So what's really holding you back?

It's a mind game. If your mind isn't in the right place, you are not prepared to win. You will continue to struggle to see the success that you greatly desire.

My goal with this book is to help you change the way that you think. This is real talk for real life. Before we start, I ask, "Are you ready to win?"

Round 1
Who's that girl?

> *I'm every woman. It's all in me.*
> *- Chaka Khan*

Obviously, I am not every woman, I am not you, and you are not me. I just really like that song! But, chances are, we struggle with some of the same issues.

So, who am I?

I am a girl whose life began in the projects on the South Side of Chicago. My mother was 17 years old, and my father was 18. My parents were high school sweethearts who never married and separated shortly after I was born. I am thankful for the fact that I was blessed with a strong mother, and that she had strong family support.

When it was time to enroll me in school, my young mother did her best. I recall as a four- or five-year-old testing for many schools. They said that I am pretty smart, so I was being tested to be part of a program for gifted students. I remember how I felt when I heard that I was accepted into the Walt Disney Magnet School. I was so excited! That school was beautiful. I still remember walking the halls, or at least I think I still remember. I could be imagining that. Anyway, the Walt Disney School ended up being way too far away, so I did not go there. Instead, I attended Holy Angels, a Catholic school not too far from our home. The school was close by, but far enough that I was exposed to a totally different element. I was sad.

At five years old, though, I didn't have much of a choice. So, Holy Angels it was! The school wasn't so bad, but we had the ugliest uniforms! They were brown and white plaid. How unfashionable! I did well at school, and I really began to enjoy it there. Some of my best friends today are from Holy Angels. It was at H.A. (that's what we call it) that, at the young age of seven or eight, I first began to feel that I was not enough. I was a skinny kid with short hair and, often times, I was teased about being skinny. Also, here I was at this Catholic school with all of these children who had both a mother and father at home. They lived in houses and had cars. That was the opposite of my life. I was ashamed of living in the projects, so I made up a story about living in this place near my home that I deemed to be nicer.

At school, I was ashamed of where I lived but, when I got home, the kids in our community didn't care for me because I wasn't like them. I didn't go to their schools, I talked "proper," and I didn't like to do the things that they liked to do for fun. This made me feel isolated, and I became a loaner. I retreated into a world of my own. I believe this was where my vivid imagination grew.

At an early age I had developed the ability to create my own reality. This ability stayed with me. In third grade, due to an unfortunate turn of events, I had to leave Holy Angels. So I transferred to a new school.

Again, I was devastated. And, again, I created a world of my own to make my transition easier.

At this new school, I decided to tell people that I was cousins with Michael Jordan. This was, in fact, true. I had a cousin named Michael and my family name was Jordan. However, my cousin, Michael, did not play for the Chicago Bulls. I really had convinced my classmates and teachers that I was related to a celebrity. In retrospect, my teachers could probably see right through my story, but the kids all wanted to hang out with me. I had a following. I had learned to cope by living in a faux reality, and it has been a constant source of comfort for me whenever things got too hard to bear.

As I got older, the stories were not as elaborate and, often times, they were not shared publicly. I lived in a reality inside of my own head. As a result of feeling ashamed and afraid, I developed the ability to stop "feeling." I am not sure exactly at what age this happened but, at some point, I learned how to be a machine.

By the time I was 17, I was attending my second high school, once again far away from my comfort zone. I hated it there. The school was located in the suburbs of Chicago, which was far away from everyone that I knew. All the kids at my new school had already formed friends, and many of them had attended school together their entire lives. Like before, I did not fit in. I wasn't really good at making new friends, so I did what came natural to me - I retreated back to my old friends. I hopped on public transportation and headed into the city to meet my crew every chance I could. My crew was where I could be me. We began to hang out, drink cheap liquor, and miss school. Before long, I was pregnant, and so was one of my best friends. Here we are, two "good girls" from Catholic school, pregnant by guys from the neighborhood. This was a very scary time, but I didn't have time to feel the fear. I had to get to action. No one knew that I was pregnant, and I planned on keeping it that way for as long as I could. Here is where my "smarts" came in handy. I was able to do some research (I'm not sure how, since there was no Google then) and found a doctor so that I could receive prenatal care. I enrolled in a program to receive benefits from the government and, most importantly, I was able to hide my pregnancy by wearing my boyfriend's clothes. Thank God the 90s was a decade of oversized clothing!

As to be expected, eventually everyone found out that I was pregnant, and life went on. I had a bouncing baby girl my senior year of high school. Having a baby did not slow me down one bit. In fact, I graduated high school early! I was a machine. After graduating, I went to work, and later started college. When my daughter was a little over one year old, her father, my then boyfriend, committed suicide. Whoa! Talk about being dealt a blow. What's a girl to do? I was a machine. I kept it moving. Enter the new faux reality.

At this phase in my life, I became extremely aloof and super independent. I could do anything I wanted. Boyfriends were disposable, and college was a waste of time. I quit college and got a full time job. I changed boyfriends quite a bit. When I did have a boyfriend, if he required too much of me, he had to go. I never became attached. Like I said, at this point, boyfriends were disposable. This phase lasted for a few years. Eventually I got a boyfriend and kept him. You're probably thinking that this guy must have been super special and a knight in shining armor, right? Nope! I mean, he wasn't a bad guy, but the experience was not life changing. Well, I guess it was, since I had my second daughter with him, and we got married, in that order (backwards, as usual, for me).

Fast forward a few years later. I now have the job that I thought would elevate my life. The salary was great, especially for a young wife and mother. There were people who worked with me that had been with the company since before I was born, and had been able to raise their families with a good life. I should be ecstatic, but I'm not. Ever heard the phrase, "More money, more problems?" I lived it. I had some of my worst experiences working that job. What made it really bad was that I couldn't quit because we needed the money and, with no education, the chances of me making that type of money again were slim. But, hey, I was a machine! I wanted to start my own business, work for myself and run shit. So I did.

I started my first official business in 2006. I grabbed two creative girls from work, and we set out to start a tee shirt line. "Heart 'n Sole Boutique" was born. I remember sitting in Pizza Hut with my girls and talking through ideas. We decided to go with cool designs on tees that related to shoes. What girl doesn't love shoes, right? The partnership did not evolve, and the tee shirt line was put on hold.

By now you know that I am a machine, so the tee shirt line didn't go away. I just had to figure out how to do it by myself. After some research, I was able to get the shirts designed and printed. Around this time, entrepreneurship was pretty popular with my age group. Through Myspace (remember Tom and Myspace?), I was able to connect with some like-minded people, and found a web developer. With tee shirts in hand, my friends and family went with me to the park and began taking pictures for the new website. Viola! We did it! The website was up, and I was in business. Only problem is, I never sold one item from the website. There was that faux reality again. I believed that I could start a business just because I wanted to. I believed that, because I liked this concept, others would, too. Boy, was I wrong!

I was no quitter, though. I just needed to figure out how to make it work. Hmmm... maybe tee shirts alone weren't enough to get people to buy. I thought about it, and I decided to order more clothes and accessories to sell. I now had an online boutique! Only problem is, again, I never sold one item from the boutique.

I was no quitter, though. The online store didn't work because people did not know about it. So, what do you do next? You open a brick and mortar location, naturally! I figured, "Hey, people always compliment me on what I am wearing, so naturally they will buy from me". That was pretty much all of the thought I put into it. The next day, I was up and at it. I convinced the salon owner where I got my hair done to let me rent the front of her salon. I went online, found places to order clothes wholesale, located a local place where I could buy women's accessories at a wholesale rate and, viola! I had a boutique. Within 30 days of my bright idea, my store was open. Awesome, right? WRONG! I failed to mention that I still had that full time job, so I couldn't reasonably run a boutique. Dilemma number one: I needed to hire someone. Where would I find someone? I didn't have any money to pay an employee. Also, what hours will the boutique be open?

Luckily, I found someone willing to work the hours that I needed, for what I could afford to pay. Great, right? Wrong, again! The person I hired had absolutely no sales experience, did not know how to set up or close down a store (neither did I), and they did not dress or present themselves in the way I wanted my boutique's image to reflect. Deep sigh. I figured I could work around this. I just needed a body in the space. The items would sell themselves, considering the patrons of the salon had to walk through the boutique to get to the salon, right? Wrong, AGAIN! Not only did the items not sell themselves, they actually grew legs and started walking out of the boutique! My employee did not give a darn about my inventory; therefore, they weren't monitoring it. When I came to the store to check inventory, many items were missing, and there was no cash in exchange for them.

You can imagine my frustration at this point. Even though there was no cash for the inventory missing, the rent still needed to be paid, the employee still needed to be paid for their time AND I needed to buy more inventory. Where would this money come from? It came from my weekly paycheck. My husband was not too happy about that little detail. I ended up letting the employee go and hiring another who was better at sales. However, this person needed to bring their child to work with them (I can't make this stuff up)! Being the inexperienced business person I was, I agreed to this. I'm sure I do not need to tell you this situation did not end well. As you can probably guess, I closed the boutique and took a loss.

I was back to the job I hated with no outlet, and I became extremely frustrated. I believe that, during that time, I suffered from depression. However, true to form, I was a machine, so kept going. I did this for a couple of years until it got to the point where I simply could not function in that space any longer. I had to do something different.

Why did I keep failing? Why was I repeating the same cycle over and over? The problem was not just that I was unprepared. And it was not that I didn't have what it takes. The problem was that I was not prepared to win. I had many barriers standing in between me and success. If I suspect correctly, so do you. That's the reason why I am sitting down to write this book.

Over the next few chapters I want to talk about some of the ways that we as women can prepare ourselves to win.

So, grab your favorite drink, a pen, and a notebook, and let's get to it!

Do what you do best; if you are a runner, run, if you're a bell, ring.
-Ignas Bernstein

Round 2

Cleaning out My Closet

Free your mind and the rest will follow.

-EnVogue

Clutter is defined as "a collection of things lying about in an untidy mass." Simply put, it means full of junk! Usually, when you think of clutter, you think of a room filled with things, or that pesky junk drawer that everyone has. But clutter can also be mental or emotional. When you have several thoughts racing through your head, and you are not able to turn off and relax or meditate, you have mental clutter. Do you find it difficult to focus on the task at hand or what's happening in the present moment because you are busy thinking about the worries of yesterday and stressing over tomorrow? This is mental clutter.

In order to be a winner, you must be able to focus. Winning requires complete dedication to the goal ahead. Ever hear the term "tunnel vision"? This is when you are so focused on where you are headed that you are not able to see what's around you. Now, you don't necessarily have to be that blinded, but you must be able to hone in on where you are trying to go.

What are some of the causes of mental clutter? Regrets, frustration, anger, anxiety and self-doubt are all causes of mental clutter. Perhaps you are holding on to the anger of something that happened to you as a child, or maybe you are upset because you were passed over for a promotion. You may be hurt because a spouse cheated on you, or you are feeling unsure of yourself because you haven't lost the "baby weight" yet. While these are valid reasons to be upset and have strong emotions, holding on to these feelings of hurt, disappointment, and resentment will keep you from receiving the joy that life has to offer.

You must let go of those ill thoughts and feelings. Mental clutter will not vanish on its own one day. To clear the mental clutter, you must face it. You have to face it to fix it. Stop burying the pain or putting it on the backburner. Pushing those thoughts to the back of your mind is eating away at you slowly, like a cancer. I am sure you have seen instances where these negative thoughts have reared themselves when you least expected it. Don't think so? Let me refresh your memory. Remember that day when you woke up really grumpy, snappy and edgy? This was probably related to a form of mental clutter which kept you from resting while you slept. Ever just feel blue when everyone else is happy, like around the holidays? That's mental clutter.

So how do get started clearing your mind? Analyze the issue. If you can't put your finger on the cause right away, try this: sit in a room in silence with your eyes closed for 20 minutes. Sit completely still and clear your mind. If you cannot clear your mind, make note of the thoughts that are going through your head. Jot them down. After you take a break, try it again. If your mind is still racing, write some more. Rinse and repeat (do this again) until you feel your mind begin to stop racing and calm down.

Once you finally get your thoughts to rest, look at the notes you have written down. Now it's time to "assess the mess." Take a clean sheet of paper and make columns. Try starting with three or four columns. Sort through the thoughts that you have written down and group them according to how easily you can resolve the issue.

Here is an example of how to do this:

Mind Clutter

Laundry, grocery store, need to take dog to vet, need new car, must save $$, upset because mom is sick, hate my job, feeling fat, scared I will look silly when I dance at the wedding, mad at my mom for being at work all the time, my uncle used to touch me and I never told a soul, I need to study for this test, I want to watch my favorite show, need to pay the cable bill what size shoes does dad wear, have to get him a gift, I wonder how to make cheesecake.

Even by using this visual aid, you can see how all of these thoughts leave little room for anything else. After you have jotted down the thoughts, group them into categories. Feel free to use whatever categories fit for you.

Here is an example of grouping:

Things I can fix this week	Things I can prepare to fix	Things I may need help with	Things I cannot control/ but I can change my thoughts
Laundry, grocery, pay cable bill, get dad's gift and find out what size shoe he wears, study for test	Save money, get new car, scared that I will look silly dancing at wedding, hate my job, learn to make cheesecake, feeling fat	Mad at mom for working all the time, my uncle used to touch me and I never told a soul	Mad because mom is sick

Now it's time to face the facts and do the work. Look at the items on your list, and determine what you need to do to resolve them. Make a "to do" list. The goal is to completely remove or, at minimum, reduce your mind of clutter. Figure out what you can do. Do you need to make calls to friends or family to express your feelings? Should you locate a mental health professional and make an appointment for help working through some of the tougher issues? Do you need to start looking for a new job?

Now that you know what you need to do, map out your plan. Look at a calendar and begin to put date on each task. This gives a specific timeline by which you will deal with this issue.

Once you have addressed and resolved the issue, let it go! Do not let old issues haunt you, even if you cannot completely rid yourself of a situation.

Commit to changing the way that you deal with the stressor. Don't let all those bad feelings take up space in your head again. Make it a point to practice noting situations that upset you, and quickly resolve the situation.

After you have cleared the mental clutter, develop healthy ways to keep all that junk from piling up again. Life will inevitably come with stress. How you deal with it is what makes the difference.

There are several methods that you may use to assist you in preventing mental clutter.

Try one or all of them:

Yoga
Meditation
Physical activity
Drawing or painting
Journaling
Listening to music
Praying
Reading

Remember, you are in control of what takes up residence in your head. Arm yourself with healthy habits to clear the clutter before it piles up again.

Round 3

The Mind of a Champion

> *I came to win, to rise to conquer.*
> *-Rihanna*

Now that you have cleared the clutter, it's time to plan for winning. As women, we struggle with many insecurities. Oftentimes we do not believe that we are enough. This self-doubt is also a pathway to self-sabotage. We have to rid ourselves of this self-destructive behavior. If you want to win you must move your minds from pain to gain.

Signs of Pain Brain	Signs of Gain Brain (the winning mindset)
Feelings of fear, boredom, and feeling stuck.	Sense of adventure, growth, and confidence.

What are you telling yourself?

Have you ever heard or told a lie so good that you believed it, even though you knew that it was a lie? That is the power of the human mind. You can persuade yourself to believe anything!

You are the person that you are today because of what you believe. With that being said, you must stop telling yourself negative things aloud or subconsciously. Stop the negative self-talk, the self-sabotage and the self-defeat. Remove "I can't," and stop believing that you are "less than." This is just simply untrue. You are lying to yourself. You can do whatever you believe. If you must lie to yourself, tell yourself good lies! Speak it until it becomes real, fake it until you make it and say it until you see what you have said.

Get in the mirror every day and say, "I will not accept defeat! I came to win, and I will win one way or another!"

Nika Corbett of "30 days of Positivity" tells us a few things to give up if, in fact, we plan to reach our goals.

We need to give up:

1. Self-Doubt - Do not talk yourself out of it before you begin. I have seen many people do this. They set a goal and, in the same breath, they say, "That's too big," "I can't do it," or "Let me go smaller!" Do not do this. You can do what you put your mind to. You can literally amaze yourself.

2. Thoughts of Failure - You can do this! Do not think failure, think improvement. If you fall a tad bit short, use that as a stepping stone. Don't stop. Don't give up. Do better the next day.

3. Fear of Success - Sounds odd, right? Some of us are secretly scared to succeed. Some are afraid of the responsibility that comes with success, scared of the changes that success brings, and they fear they are not ready for success. Do not discount yourself! You are more than able and, as a matter of fact, you deserve to be successful!

Goals are like flowers and plants. To realize their beauty, you must nurture the goals. Treat your goals like plants, and watch what happens!

What exactly does that mean? Let's look at the process of a plant.

First, you must FERTILIZE the soil for the plant to grow. The same applies to your goal or dream. You must start with an open mind. Accept the possibility of reaching this goal, and accept the reality of succeeding.

Once you have fertilized the soil, it's time to PLANT the seed. Planting the seed means that you understand what you are attempting to do. Be clear, specific, and intentional.

Once you know your goal, say it out loud. Say it again. Write it down. Tell a friend. This makes it real, and puts it into the universe. Every day speak your goal out loud to yourself. Speak it as though it is. Make yourself believe that YOU WILL DO THIS because, I am here to tell you, you can, and you will.

It's time to GERMINATE. This is when you strategize. How will you reach your goal? What steps do you need to take to make this a reality? Create your blueprint. Nothing will work without a plan, and you also need a "pivot plan." This needs to be in place so that when you run into roadblocks, you do not give up. You will have an idea on how to handle the road block without becoming overwhelmed.

Now watch your plant GROW. You have planted the seed, so it's time to make it grow. This is your action phase. Move on the steps that need to be accomplished. Start small and work your way up. Check things off the list, and celebrate the small successes. You deserve it!

Multiply! Do it all again. Success breeds success. Once you have accomplished your goal, celebrate yourself, and then set another one. Rinse and repeat. This is how you win. Once you have mastered or conquered one level or skill, then move to the next level, and conquer that.

Set goals. Reach goals. Set new goals.

Repeat!

Round 4

Don't worry, I will wait.

Today I don't feel like doing anything. I just want to lay in my bed
- Bruno Mars

You struggle with procrastination. That is something that many of us women deal with on a regular basis. For a better understanding, let's take a quick look at its definition.

Procrastination means "the avoidance of doing a task which needs to be accomplished." It is "the practice of doing more pleasurable things in place of less pleasurable ones, or carrying out less urgent tasks instead of more urgent ones, thus putting off impending tasks to a later time."

When you look at this definition, it would seem as if procrastinating is literally "wasting your time." It's being busy doing nothing. Why do we do this? Why would we rather spend time doing things that are not helping us to reach our goals, instead of doing things that help us get there?

The definition says that one would rather do more "pleasurable things." Girl, I totally understand this one! Why would I want to go to the dentist, when I can go to the mall? The mall is so much more fun! Well, that works until that one day when I wake up at 2:00 am with the worst toothache EVER!

Now, instead of just needing the filling that I avoided three months ago, my entire tooth is cracked, and I need to have it pulled. Ouch! Guess I will be calling up the dentist now, and rushing them to get me in.

As you see in my example, when you procrastinate, it can often make the issue bigger, and the problem more stressful. I am pretty sure you know this already.

So why do you struggle with continuously procrastinating? If you are like me, I like to believe that I do my best work under pressure. I am the person who starts a project the night before it is due and still ace it. I will most likely be extremely tired the next day but, hey, that is the price that you pay. Well, the problem with this is that it leaves no room for error. What if something does not work as expected? I am, (I mean we are), pretty much screwed. This adds to my/our stress level. Also, I'm certain that I/we can perform tasks well with more time available than the final hour. So again, why do I/we wait until the last minute?

Let's look a little deeper into your daily life.

Do you often pay your bills on the due date or late?
Do you miss out on the early bird specials?
Are you out on Christmas Eve doing your shopping?
No judgement. I do all of the above too.

Procrastination is really a form of self-sabotage, and an issue with self-regulation. Oftentimes we over-estimate how much time we have, and under-estimate how much time it will take to get done the things that we need to do. Do you see the conflict?

Studies tell us that procrastinators are not born, they are made. You can stop saying, "I am just this way," because you are not. Even though you were not born a procrastinator, your parents may have had a lot to do with the fact that you are one.

Can you think of when procrastination became a problem for you? Many of us who are procrastinators grew up in strict homes or places with set rules, such as catholic schools, which is the case for me. We did not have to self-regulate, we were told what to do and when to do it. So as we got older, we rebelled. We decided we would get to it when we get to it. This was the beginning of the procrastinating ways.

The actual reason that we procrastinate is that the task at hand is uncomfortable for us. It may bring about some sort of pain. We do not want to feel this. Think about the tasks that you tend to procrastinate with. Think about how you feel at the thought of completing that task. I'm almost willing to bet something about completing that task was uncomfortable for you.

Don't believe me. Let's look!

Why are you waiting until Christmas Eve to shop, when Christmas is the same day every year? You might hate shopping. You may lack the money. You might hate to wrap gifts. All of those are pain points for you.

Why do you wait to type your paper until the day before its due? You may not be confident in the work. You may hate to read the chapters. It might take you a long time to put your thoughts together. More pain points.

As adults we procrastinate in many ways that we may not even realize. Can't stay away from Facebook, Twitter and Instagram? These are huge time stealers. Are you always checking your email? I know you don't want to miss that one important message, but is it really that urgent? What you are actually doing is retreating to a place of comfort. These things do not bring you stress and pain. They feel good, and that is why you run to them.

Typically there are 3 types of procrastinators:

1. The Thrill Seeker - This is me. I am the person who likes the rush of doing things at the last minute.

2. The Avoider - This is the person who does not want to deal with the issues at hand. Many times this is a manifested form of fear.

3. The Decisional Procrastinator - This is the person who just cannot make a decision. Secretly they believe that, if they do not decide, then they are not responsible for the outcome. NEWSFLASH! That is not true! Not deciding is the same as deciding!

Which one do you most identify with?

I hate to be the bearer of bad news, but procrastination causes more stress. It can affect your health if this way of living is maintained. Therefore, we must rid ourselves of this pesky little habit. Sounds great right? I'm sure your question now is, "How do you stop the madness," right?

The good news is that procrastination can be overcome. I won't lie and say that it is easy, but it is possible.

Here is what top researchers say we can do:

1. Recognize when you are procrastinating. Make note of the things that you do to avoid completing your task at hand. This will help you to recognize when you are procrastinating.

2. As I pointed out earlier, we procrastinate to avoid pain. Identify the pain that the task will cause you. What are you running from?

3. You must decide if this task is something that you are going to do. If you decide not to scrap it all together, then you must act.

4. Bribe yourself. Give yourself a reward for completing your task sooner rather than later.

5. Under-estimate the time you have. If you have a project due tomorrow, make a note on your calendar that it is due today.

6. Be mindful of the time spent on things. Make a note of when you start and check your progress in 15-30 minute increments so you can gage how long it actually takes to get this done.

Remember that procrastination is self-sabotage. Keep that at the front of your mind. As a matter of fact, write it down, and put it some place where you can see it daily.

You are enough, and you have what it takes. Get to it!

Round 5
Love and Success

Smart enough to make these millions
Strong enough to bear the children
Then get back to business
-Beyoncé

Your relationship is strained because you are out here crushing your goals, huh?
The mister is a bit angry because you are not there to spend time with the kids?
He is also trippin' because you are acting too bossy?
Yes, this is a tough one. It is very hard to be an ambitious woman while still being a wife and mother. This requires serious effort. You have to focus on balance, and the two of you have to have an understanding.
When you say that your relationship is strained, let's talk about it.
What is the problem?
Is the issue that you somehow feel that your husband is less because he earns less?
Does your husband feel as if he is not valued?
Is your family in need of more time from you?
As a mother who works long hours outside of the home to provide for your family, you have shifted the traditional family dynamic. Our brains are naturally programmed for predefined roles. The man is the bread earner, the protector, and the head of the household. The woman is the support system

and the nurturer of the family. What happens when this is not the case?

Initially, we are not sure how to respond. Our brains are confused on how we should perform. It's a very delicate situation, and the solution varies from relationship to relationship.

For the sake of discussion I'll touch on the issues above.

For scenario one I will assume your spouse is working, but earning less.

Do you feel that your husband is less than because he earns less than you? If so, I will tell you that respect is not tied to money. Somehow I believe that money is not the issue. Look at the man realistically. If money was not a factor, how would you gage your relationship with him? Is he meeting your emotional needs? Does he stroke you mentally, intellectually and physically? Does he support you? Is he a help meet? Does he protect you from harm? Does he value your heart? Chances are your real problem is in one of those areas.

If your man cares for all of those needs, and you are still angry because he makes less than you, there is another issue.

Could it be money? If so, why is money so important? Is your brain reverting back to traditional thinking? Does he need to earn more to be the provider? Or is the issue actually that you want him to aim higher? Are you not comfortable with his ambition?

These are conversations that you and your partner need to sort through. Sometimes one party walks around angry because they are not aware of what the other party is thinking.

I was watching an episode of the TV show "Being Mary Jane" (don't judge me), and in this episode one of the successful ladies was talking to her less successful (in her opinion) ex-husband. They had two school-aged sons. The wife was a top television producer who worked crazy hours and the ex-husband was a struggling writer. She was responsible for all of the family's financial needs. At this point they were divorced and co-existing in one house, in the best interest of the children. One day she asked her ex-husband, "How did you get here?" She said, "I know how I got here, but how did you get here?" His response was so thought provoking. He said something to the fact of "this is where I wanted to be." He went on to say that "my goals were not the same as yours. You wanted to be a top producer and rule the world. I didn't. If I wasn't me, then you couldn't be you."

Think about that ladies.

Marinate on it.

If you are a wife and mom and you are out there conquering the world, who is home with your kids? Is it their dad? If so, then he is your help meet. That tidbit aside, this is the point: they had never communicated what they wanted from life. She

married a guy whose ambition level was less than hers and she did not know it. She assumed that he wanted the same things she did, and he didn't.
Their deal breaker was lack of communication. They could have avoided a lot of heartbreak by being more honest with each other. Don't assume. Talk it out.
If you all are unable to come to a happy place, it might be time to let it go. We'll discuss that more in detail in another chapter.
For scenario two, we will assume that your husband feels like he is not being valued.
Is he acting out, always angry and upset?
Do you often forget that he is a man, and that he has needs also?
Why is he feeling undervalued?
If we take a look back at our "Being Mary Jane" story, the wife failed to realize how valuable her husband was to her success. He said it plainly: "If I was not me, than you could not be you." Wow! Though I highly doubt any woman grew up with dreams of having a house husband, the role can be essential. The problem comes in when there is not an agreement, or a mutual understanding, that this is what works for your family. Sometimes people overlook things. In the example mentioned above, she did not realize the huge contribution that her husband made to her success. He freed her from worrying about her children being properly cared for as she climbed the proverbial Mt. Everest. He

deserved a little respect for that, and maybe a few other "perks" that his wife could provide!

Two things could have probably caused this situation to go wrong:

1. The wife didn't actually plan to have a house husband, and did not want one.

2, The husband did not plan to be a house husband, but he fell into the role in an effort to support his wife.

Either of these situations can cause resentment. Again, if you want to be in the relationship, you both need to talk it through and work together to create an arrangement that works for everyone involved.

For scenario three, let's say your family needs more of your time.

Well, conquering the world is not easy, and it is time consuming. What do they want from you? This world can't conquer itself!

I have a secret to share with you. Your children can't raise themselves, either. Your husband didn't get married to be alone. Your boyfriend will not continue to be your boyfriend if you are not there. You have to prioritize. I know that it may sound mundane, but you have to schedule in family time. You cannot realistically be gone for months on end if you have a husband and kids. If you do this, you will be replaced. Maybe you are okay with that. If so, then you're good. If not, you need to fix the situation.

When I say that you will be replaced, I do not necessarily mean your mate will find a new woman, even though he may. However, your kids may become more comfortable with their new nanny, or whoever provides the bulk of their care, than they are with you.

Is this a problem for you? What are you willing to do to change it?

Don't roll your eyes at me! I am all for girl bosses and girl power. I love Beyonce's song "Girls Run the World" but, in reality, even Bey has to spend some time with her husband and daughter.

I am not saying to cancel all of your meetings and trips, and tell your boss that you have to be off every day at 5 pm, but we have to cut back somewhere, ladies.

Tips that I have received regarding this issue, and things that have shown to work, are:

1. Being home and present at least one full weekend a month. No work, only family time and rest.

2. Use technology. Once a day squeeze in an hour just for your kids when you are not home. Skype and FaceTime them to hear about their day. You need this as much as they do.

3. Keep it spicy with the mister. He still has needs, even when you travel. If you don't meet these needs, I can almost promise you that there is a single mom

at your kids' school watching him who will. Again, use technology. You have to stay connected.

4. When you are home, turn off your computer and mobile devices. Be present. Try to do this every day at a certain time, or at least a couple days a week at a certain time.

5. Make time for your kids' important events.

6. Leave love notes for your family to let them know that you are thinking of them. Can you imagine how a frustrated husband's day can turn around when he finds a note of appreciation from his wife tucked in a coat pocket?

Success and relationships require balance and constant communication. I'm not claiming it to be easy, but it is possible.

Don't feel guilty about your ambition, but also don't forget that there are people in your life that are just as important as your success.

Notes

Round 6
Maintenance Needed

> *This girl needs more than occasional hugs and a token of love*
> *-Karyn White*

I always get the short end of the stick. Every morning I'm up at 6:30 am, and I don't need to be anywhere until 10 am. However, I have to get up and showered before anyone else is up. I have to get breakfast ready before the house wakes up. Then, I need to wake up the kids so they can eat, get them dressed, and off to school. I need to make sure my boyfriend has clean socks for work. I have to run by my mom's house and change her voicemail, and then I need to stop at the grocery store to make sure there is something for dinner. Oh, did I mention that I do have to go to work today as well? I am so frustrated!

Today is not a good day. Dad is sick, so we need to go by and check on him. James is tired of his dead-end job, and has decided to go back to school. He says that we will finally get married once he completes these classes. I need to make a dish for the party at my friend's house, and I don't even feel like going because I am tired. But I know she will kill me if I don't make it. Oh, goodness! Tiff is calling again. I forgot to call her back yesterday. Hey, Tiff....

Either of these sound like a typical week for you? For women most of us our days are filled with caring for others. It's typical for us to be the nurturer and be supportive of everyone else and their needs, wants and dreams.

But, what about you?

Where do you fall on your priority list?

What about your needs, wants and dreams?

They define a part of love as putting other people's needs ahead of your own. I call bull! Don't you love yourself? Why are you not taking care of you?

If you have ever traveled on an airplane, then you've heard that, in the event of an emergency, you should put on your own oxygen mask FIRST, not on your child, your husband, your mother, or your neighbor. You come first.

This shocks most people, but why is that the case? If you do not put on your mask and you die, then what good will you be to the others on the ride with you?

We need to take this same approach in our day to day lives. I am not saying to be totally selfish even though, at times, you will have to choose YOU. I am saying to tell yourself that your needs are just as important as everyone else.

Say it to yourself now out loud: "My needs are as important as everyone else!"

That's all. No additional explanation needed. Say it every day until you believe it. This may be another one that you want to write down and put it some place where you can see it.

If we consistently put ourselves last, we can end up really hurting ourselves and everyone around us. I'll use myself as an example.

If you would have met me six years ago, I was at the top of my game. Hair was always done, nails on point, dressed in the latest fashions. I was launching a business, had a good job, nice cars, a nice house, a husband, two daughters, and two pups. I was, by some standards, living the dream. I was living life on my terms, for the most part, and it felt pretty good. Then life changed. Due to a few turn of events, life as I knew it was no more. I was a full time business owner. Slowly my hair appointments spaced further and further apart. My time with friends decreased. I wasn't shopping for clothes as often. I was just trying to stay afloat, and keep the family going. Money wasn't the problem, it was my motivation. There was just no time for me. I had clients and kids to tend to. Subconsciously, I slipped into a routine of doing what everyone else needed. I was a fixer, a mom, a wife, a daughter, a sister, a business owner, and a chauffeur. I was no longer me. One day I looked up, and I hadn't seen the inside of a hair or nail salon in over a year. None of my clothes fit anymore, and I was not a happy woman. I had stopped doing what I needed to do to take care of me. My cute jeans, tops and heels were replaced by sweats, t-shirts, baseball caps and running shoes (and none of it was the cute kind). I really didn't feel like getting dressed. I just did what I had to do to get by. This is another period in my life where I think that I may have been depressed.

I barely hung out with my daughters, and I did not want to talk with my husband or friends. I was just going through the motions, muddling my way through life. Most things were still being done, but they were marginal, at best.

How do we let this happen? We forget about us. Women are hardwired to care for others, so when we see a need, we jump in to help. However, we forget that we need to help ourselves, too.

Before you fall into the abyss, or if you need to climb out of the abyss, understand that you matter. You have to let go of the desire to please people. People pleasing is a form of co-dependency.

You have to stop needing to be needed, and start taking care of yourself by setting boundaries.

You also have to know what you want, and be willing to own your truth. Once you decide what you want to do, commit to it. Commit to your wishes just like you commit to everything else. Let others carry some of the load. You'll be surprised how much your husband and kids can do if you only let them.

Stop being superwoman! Your assistant is capable. That is why you hired her.

Stop being a perfectionist. It's holding you back.

Stop sweating the small stuff! Life will go on if your kids eat fast food every once in awhile.
Give up the guilt! You deserve to be happy, too. As the old saying goes, "If mommy isn't happy, nobody's happy!" That is the truth.

Commit to you.

Grab that notepad you should already have handy, and write down one thing that you want for you. Then, write down five things that you need to do to make that happen. Finally write down one thing that you can do today to move in that direction.
It's time for action!

My best friend is the one who brings out the best in me.
-Henry Ford

Round 7

Eyes on the Target

> *Don't bother me, I'm working*
>
> *-Puff Daddy*

I struggle with focus. I remember seeing this post on Facebook that stated "If you ever want to know what a creative person's mind feels like, imagine having a browser with 2,857 tabs open ALL the time." Does that sound about right to you? When I read it, I literally laughed out loud, because that is the story of my life. I jump around quite often, finding myself literally working on 2-3 projects simultaneously.
In this world of immediacy, it is so easy to get distracted from the task at hand. In the previous decade, everything was about multitasking, getting more done quicker. Trying to be more efficient with our time. Of course, it was discovered that multitasking was much less effective than originally thought. My daughter did a full science project on the subject, and even her small scale result concluded that when we multitask, we suck!
This is the problem we encounter when we lack focus. We end up doing a whole lot of nothing.
Let me ask you a question.
How many unfinished projects do you have on your desk?
How many more around your house?
How many random ideas do you have in the notes of your phone?

I know that was more than one question. Sorry! I have a hard time focusing! :-)

You don't have to my answer questions aloud, but I know that your answer to each is probably more than two, like 5-10.

Why is that?

Of course, you could have an undiagnosed case of ADHD or ADD. I am not joking. Sometimes I really think this may be the case with me. They say that many adults are diagnosed around the age of 38. Provided that has been ruled out, some of the other reasons for lacking focus are:

1. Too much technology. Like I mentioned before, we live in a world of immediacy, where everything is literally at your fingertips. Reading an article on your Ipad and have a question? You can look at your phone and Google the answer. Since you're on the internet anyway, may as well stop over to Facebook and see what all of your friends are up to. Oh, look! A story about a new shoe store opening soon. You naturally click the link, and now you are shopping for shoes. Whew! After all that shoe shopping, you better check your bank account! You open your bank account app and look at your damage. Just then, you realize that you haven't paid the light bill. Better do that before you are in the dark. Oh, that reminds me! I wanted to return some candles to Target. Let me get up and get dressed. And just like that, you are completely pulled away from what you were doing.

2. You're not getting enough rest. If you do not have the proper rest, you will not be able to properly function. I know you remember back in school the teacher always said to get plenty of rest the night before the big test. The need for rest did not change as you grew up. You just began to neglect sleep more. This causes difficulty for staying on task.

3. You're bored. And when we are bored, we seek out excitement. If you are working on something that is tedious, it is easy to find something else more interesting to do. Then you end up putting the boring task to the side and start working on something that is more exciting.

I never realized how quickly I get bored with things. I recently discovered that I like the rush of creating something from nothing. I will work like crazy to get a project up and running and, once it's up, I am over it. I toss it to the side like toys after Christmas. On to the next thrill for me.

4. You feel defeated. If you worked hard on a project only to receive poor reviews from a client or boss, you may become discouraged with that project, and move to something fresh to re-ignite your flame. Whether we like to admit it or not, we want to feel good and be proud of our work. If we are shot down, we can find ourselves moving to something that will provide us with more positive feedback.

5. You are stressed. You literally have too much on your mind. Scientifically speaking, stress slows down

the thinking process, thus making it hard to focus. Stress can also make you sick. Some of the biggest effects of stress are headaches and lethargy. When you are not feeling your best, it is easy to get distracted and put off doing things that are important.

I'm sure at one point or another you have suffered from one, or many, of these distractors. Lacking focus is not a fun thing and, at times, it can even be frustrating. You may feel as if you are spinning your wheels and are stuck.

Lack of focus is a HUGE time waster,

There are techniques that can help you with your focus. "Help" is the key word, because being focused is either a medical or discipline issue. If it is not medical, then it is up to you to work the techniques and make them work.

Here are a few tips for better focus:

1. Unplug. I can see you twitching right about now. It's okay. When you turn back on your devices, all the messages, statuses and posts will still be there. Turn off all electronic devices except for anything that is essential to you completing the task at hand.

2. If you can, revert back to paper and pen/pencil, and work that way. The internet is a very tempting place, so stay clear.

3. Set up times each day where no technology is permitted. Give your mind a break from constantly staring at the computer.

4. Get some much-needed rest. Try to make sure that you are in bed at a decent time. When you can sneak it in, go to bed a little earlier and sleep a little later.
5. Prioritize your projects and pick your optimal peak time to work on those things that require the most energy. Tackle the most unappealing tasks during the periods that you are most alert.
6. Chill out. Find some time each day for "down time." You can use this time for yoga, meditation, reading, running, or exercising. It can be anything that allows you the opportunity to rest & reset your mind for better focus. Personally, I love to chill out with my earbuds in and get lost in the music.

An article that I read in *Entrepreneur* magazine noted that we can train our brains to focus on the task at hand.

Here some key takeaways on how to do it:

1. Allot your time. Block out times during the day that you will only work on the specific task for that period. Do not allow yourself to do anything else.
2. Practice concentration. Literally practice focusing in on one thing. Turn off all distractions and just focus. Start off doing so in small increments, then gradually increase your focus time. This practice trains your brain to focus.

3. Do real work first. Use your brain while your energy level is high. This is the optimal time to do creative things, such as writing your newsletter, or developing new projects. You can do the things that do not require much thought after you have worked on the more intense things. This gives your mind some time to rest.

Round 8
Losing Steam

Truth is I'm weak, No strength to fight
- Tamela Mann

"Truth is, I am tired! I am tired to the point of not being able to get out of bed. I can't think straight. My brain might actually be broken, and my head hurts. It's just too much, and I cannot take one more thing. Not today, please not today! Not tomorrow, either. I'll try again next week."

This is snapshot of how being burnt out can feel.

I am woman! Bring it on! Hear me roar! (Cue Katy Perry's "Eye of the Tiger.") This is how the ambitious approach life. We say, "Give it here. I can handle it, all of it. I got this."

We keep taking on task after task, project after project. We will not complain about having a heavy workload. Hell, that is what we wanted. Keep those clients coming! Being busy means that we are getting things done. Right?

Before we know it, we are working from sun up to sundown and through dinner, on the weekends, and sometimes even holidays. We are missing the kids' performances and games because we are tied to our devices. "There is no time to chat. I have work to do. Can't you see I'm busy conquering the world over here?"

Chances are, if you are working this much and this hard, you are skipping meals, you're not getting exercise and, if you work from home, you are probably skipping a shower or two (been there, done that). You're stressed and always fighting some ridiculous deadline that you are committed to.

This pace is not good. It's not healthy and, believe it or not, your body will shut down. Literally! I know women that have ended up in the hospital from over-exertion.

This, friends, is burnout!

You have no more gas, and the car just will not go any further.

This is a "code red, man down" situation!

You need to avoid burnout. Not only is it not healthy, it is also counterproductive. You are working your ass off to meet ridiculous demands. You're probably not doing your best work because you are stressed, and then you lose interest or you get sick and you can't do anything. CRASH! It all falls down. You've worked all that time to get nowhere. Talk about depressing!

Burnout is a result of poor planning and poor time management. Many women struggle with this, since we believe we are superwomen, or so we lead everyone else to believe.

Be realistic. There are only 24 hours in a day, and you will not be able to use them all working on your goals. You can stop trying now. Working until 2 am, off to bed and back up at 6 am will not get you any further. It may work for a while, but no human being can keep up at that pace. I suggest you do not start those practices.

How can you be productive, conquer the world, and still be healthy and sane? I'm glad you asked. Again, be realistic. How much can you really do?

Here are some tips to help avoid getting burned out:

1. Make a schedule. Block out times during the day, week, and month that you will not work. Create work hours for yourself, and honor them.
2. Create a plan. How long does it take for you to complete common tasks? How many of those tasks can you do during the work hours that you scheduled above?
3. Give yourself limits. Your personal time is just that. Do not give business contacts your personal email address or personal cellphone number.
4. Unplug (does that sound familiar?). Turn off all electronics for a period of time every day.
5. Get up and move. Make sure you are not sitting down all day, every day. Schedule in time for a walk. You need to get away and reset your mind. Try doing this for 20 minutes a day.

My biggest tip to avoid burnout and increase productivity is to DELEGATE!!!

This is so very important. Two heads are better than one, and four hands can achieve more than two. I know delegation is a scary thing. No one can do your stuff as good as you do. Come close...I want to whisper in your ear ,"that may or may not be true". I know that you are great, but there are probably parts in many of your projects that someone else can do, too.

What I like to tell my clients from my virtual assistant company is that there are some parts of your business that only you can do. However, there are many others that are a complete waste of your time.

One of my coaches told me that the brain (you) of the business (or home) needs to work on the money items (the most important thing). If it is not a money item, you can create a manual and teach someone else to do it.

Your task is to figure out what things only you can do. Once you decide that, the other stuff can be handed off. So, schedule some time to create manuals for someone else to follow to complete those tasks. What I suggest is that, as you perform the non-money tasks, write down step by step what you do. Look over the steps, then follow the guide you've written, EXACTLY as it is written, to make sure that you did not miss anything. Sometimes we may skip writing a step because we do it without thinking about it, which can be a critical error for your understudy.

After the manual is perfected, time to find an understudy. Spend some time thinking of what sort of person can complement your style. This is somewhat like a marriage. They don't have to be exactly like you, in fact it may be more beneficial to have someone who has more of what you lack. Don't rush the process of choosing a good understudy. Choose wisely! If not, you will have to replace them and start the process over. We are trying to be smart and productive!

For example, I'm the visionary. I see the "big picture." It is helpful for me to surround myself with detail-oriented people because they can catch the things I miss. Another way to attack this is to hire people who can do what you hate. I don't do sales. I keep someone who is good at sales on my team. I suck at Microsoft Excel, so I have a girl on my team who is the Excel guru. Get it?

Do not be afraid to have more than one person that works with you. I like to put people in the positions that they love. This way, I know they will do a superb job. This way we are all happy and doing what we love to do.

Now if you have a concern about the integrity of your product or service, I suggest delegating to someone who is a doer rather than a thinker. Sometimes you will need thinkers and, other times, you need doers.

Thinkers are those who can make decisions in your absence. They can spot holes in the strategy and fill them, or offer suggestions on how to fill them.

Doers, on the other hand, just do the job. These people are more of your "assembly line" type of people. They work best in positions that are repetitive. They just follow the template, copy and paste. They aren't really concerned with learning more about what you do. They just want to do their job.

I spoke of delegation in business terms, but this can also be applied in your personal life as well. As I stated in a previous chapter, don't underestimate the abilities of the people around you. The same rules apply. There are some things that only you can do, and the other things you can teach your spouse, siblings, neighbors and kids to do. You do not have to tackle everything. Honestly, you should not even try to. Do not be afraid to ask for help. That is not a sign of failure. It can actually be a path to success.

Round 9
Must be the Money

> *It's like the more money we come across the more problems we see*
> *-Notorious Big*

I'll be honest with you. When I started to write this chapter, I shied away several times. I clicked on over to Facebook, checked my email, texted a few friends, anything that kept me distracted from writing. I was procrastinating. Money talk makes me nervous. I have a love/hate relationship with money. I love making and spending it, but I hate managing it. Yes, a bad combination, I know. I also know that I am not alone here. PLEASE tell me that you can relate! I'll act like I heard you say, "Yes, I totally understand."

I'm glad you understand, sis!

Back when I wrote checks, I was terrible at balancing my checkbook, and I do mean TERRIBLE! Do you know how much joy I felt with the popularity of the debit card? I could stop paying all those silly overdraft fees!

Oh, and since we are talking about credit and credit cards, I remember when I thought of credit as basically gifts that the bank gave me. My credit was terrible! I was so irresponsible. I eventually realized items bought on credit were not gifts, and I had to pay for them. So I was sure to send in my $15.00 per month on the dress that cost $25.00. Again, silly!

I'm not exactly sure why I didn't get the lesson the first time. I normally learn fast, but not with money. Sigh, I guess I just liked making the banks wealthier. I'm not coming to you today as a money expert because I AM NOT! I was actually persuaded to add this chapter by my friend who is a money guru. She said, "You can't talk about winning in life and business without talking about money." I guess she is kind of right, so here we are.

Because this is my platform, and I can write whatever I want, I decided the best way I can help is to talk about the mindset and money. What do we believe about money, and why do we treat or abuse our finances the way that we do?

Money issues are bigger than not making enough money. If you think about it, those that are poor and broke are those that are rich and broke. I remember an old client of mine publicly announcing that his business brought in $600,000 a month in revenue (sounds great to me!). He went on to say that, however, they spent $750,000 a month. He said they were just broke on a high level. Damn.

Making more money does not solve your money crisis. Praying for the better paying job will not solve your problems if you do not know how to handle money. A better paying job just gives you more money to spend. You can buy more stuff, better shoes, nicer cars, and bigger houses. However, more money can cause you more problems, if you are not careful.

Your relationship with money is probably the same as your relationship with many other things.
Some questions you may want to ask yourself are:
How do you think about money?
Do you even actually THINK about money? Or, are you like how I once was, the person who thought of money as the "magical thing" that I would never run out of?
Do you believe that you are worth more money than you are making or charging? Or, can you not charge more or request a higher salary because you have deemed that you are not valued that high?
What are your money patterns?
Are you a spender, over spender or a saver?
Do you monitor the bank account, or are you afraid to check the balance?
Have you experienced accounts being closed or charged off?
Have you ever had a car repossessed? Lost a home?
Do you wait until you get the past due or shut off notice to pay?
You don't have to tell me these things, but what you do need to do is get honest with yourself about how you view money and how you feel about money.

Get to the root of your issue. What is your money mindset, and where did it come from?
Research shows that most people form their money habits from their families. I can attest to this.

Growing up we weren't rich by any means, but we always had very nice things. As a result, I grew up with a taste for nice things. Cost was never a factor for determining if I made the purchase. If I really wanted it, I bought it, whether I could afford it or not.

We can really be blinded by our upbringing. I recall when I first started living with my then boyfriend. We went grocery shopping and, as we were getting canned vegetables, I picked all of the different Del Monte brand veggies. He asked, "Why are you picking up the most expensive brand?" I responded, "Are there other kinds?" I was serious, too. We were standing in the canned goods aisle of the grocery store, and I did not notice all of the other brands that were right in front of me. I was pre-programmed for Del Monte. This was the only brand I had ever seen in my home.

I always tell that story because it was eye opening for me. I was going to pay two or three times the cost of some of the other brands, and I had no clue why.

He, on the other hand, had a very different money experience. He knew that money was finite and that it had to be used wisely. He was very mindful of dollars spent. This actually drove me nuts!

Our money experiences shaped how we view money. I believed that money will always come. He believed that you had to hold on to the money that you have. Is one money belief better than the other? Again, understanding your money belief or mindset is the key to how you handle your finances. My friend would always say if you want to win in life and business, you had better know how to handle your finances.

Now, let me reiterate. I am not a money expert, but I'll share what I've learned along the way:

First, get real honest with yourself. Be transparent about your money beliefs, money fears and your financial status.

Next, grab your notebook and really examine your money mindset. Write a short note to yourself on how you view money and why you believe that your views are as such.

Now, look at your current numbers. Write down how much is coming into your household each month, then write what is going out. Compare the amounts and adjust, if needed.

Next up is your credit. Do you know your credit score? What items are on your credit report? What are the interest rates on your outstanding debt (if you have any)?

It's time now to write down your financial goals. What would you like to purchase? How much does it cost? How much do you want/need to save? By when?

What bills do you want to pay off? By when? How much are they?

How much do you want to invest?

What do you want to leave in the event of your death? Who is going to get it?

After answering those questions, write down your action steps. This is where you list your plan to reach all of the goals that you listed in the above step. Take your time and be detailed. Think it through. If you need help, enlist the assistance of a trusted and knowledgeable person. This could be a family member or a professional.

Money matters are very personal, and it can be intimidating to think about. Nonetheless, you have to know where you are and where you want to go in order to get there. Otherwise, you are just blowing wherever the wind takes you. That, girlfriend, is not winning.

You can do this!

Change your bad money habits, and you literally change your life!

Round 10
The Blueprint

Cause I am a champion and you're gonna hear me roar

-Katy Perry

Ever wondered why some people seem to easily achieve those things that they desire, while others continue to run around on the proverbial rat wheel? It's about mindset and understanding how to set goals that are achievable. Achievable does not equate to small or easy.

In order for a goal to be achievable, it must first be clear. You must know exactly what you are trying to do. I suggest using the SMART Goals formula:

Specific - State exactly what you want to achieve. Saying, "I want to lose weight," is not a specific goal. An example of a specific goal is "I want to make $45,000 by November 13th." Having specific goals allow you to better chart a course of action to achieve them.

Measurable - You cannot improve on what you are not able to measure. Using the example above, if you want to make $45,000 by November 13th, assuming that it is 5 months from today, you can reasonably say you will need to make an average of $9,000.00 per month for the next 5 months.

Attainable and Action-Oriented - Is this goal realistic for you? Can you honestly make $9000 in one month doing what it is that you are doing? If not, then you must figure out what actions steps you need to take in order to reach this monthly milestone.

You are more than likely to stick with the goal if it is directly relevant to you and your current or future quality of life. Think about it. If you know that in order to buy a new house you will need to save $3000.00 for a down payment, this gives your goal a purpose.

Goals without timelines are dreams. Not only must your goal be measurable, it must be time-sensitive. Having a designated completion date increases urgency and decreases the likelihood of procrastination. And following this formula provides a roadmap to success, which you need in an effort to reach your destination.

So what's your strategy?

How do plan to reach your goal?

Every winner has a playbook to follow. You are not any different. Failure to plan is planning to fail.

In the previous section, you clearly identified your goal. You know where you are going. Now, how do you get there?

To devise your plan, analyze your goal, and then dissect it. What steps are necessary to achieve this goal? Start with your end goal, and work backwards. What smaller goals do you need to reach to achieve your BIG goal? These will be your "activation goals," which are smaller goals that directly flow into your bigger goals. It's like a reverse domino effect.

This is how activation goals work:

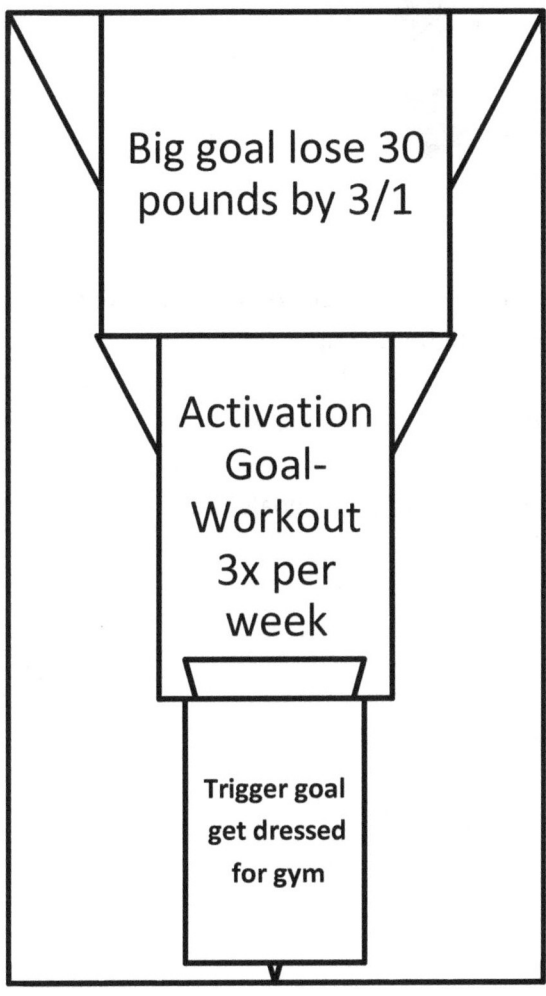

Big Goal

Activation Goal

Trigger Goal

This strategy is designed to help you take smaller bites to avoid becoming overwhelmed. By using trigger goals, you make it easier to set yourself in position to take the next step.

Trigger goals should be goals that move you to the next step.

The Final Word

You got your dreams, you got your prayers and you got your God, now go get it
-Mary Mary

Ladies,

I thank you for taking this journey with me. Writing this book has been a delight, as well as a free therapy session. Seriously!
I started writing this book two years ago, and the first two chapters (which are not chapters one and two) sat in a file on my computer for two years as I went about life. Just a little over 48 hours prior to the time I wrote this section, I was challenged to get it done in one day. Life happens, and I wasn't able to do it in 24 hours. However, it did push me. In less than two days, I completed a 13,000 word, 97 page, 10 chapter book. I say that to say that you'd be amazed at what you can do if you answer the call. If you are reading this, then that means that you have the desire to achieve success. You have the will to win and, for those two things, I applaud you. Take heed to my words: Success is personal, and you define success for yourself. Do not let anyone tell you what success should look or feel like. Do not be afraid to go full force in pursuit of those things that make you happy. You only get one life, and you should live it before you die.

Her Rules- Playlist

Intro-Ex-Factor - Lauryn Hill
Round 1 - I'm Every Woman-Chaka Khan
Round 2 - Free Your Mind-En Vogue
Round 3 - Fly - Nicki Minaj and Rihanna
Round 4 - Lazy - Bruno Mars
Round 5 - Girls Run the World - Beyoncé
Round 6 - Superwoman - Karyn Whire
Round 7 - Workin' - Puff Daddy and the Family
Round 8 - Take me to the King - Tamela Mann
Round 9 - Mo Money, Mo Problems - Notorious Big
Round 10 - Roar - Katy Perry
Final Word - Go Get Your Blessing - Mary Mary

Like what you read?

I hope that while reading this book you were able to laugh, reflect, identify, and even dance a little. Do me a favor if you enjoyed the book, if this book resonated with you, don't be shy, tell a friend, tell two. Post your favorite lines or lessons on social media. Let's keep the conversation going using the hashtag **#HERRULES**.

Be sure to connect with me on Twitter @itislatashanic and tell me what you thought of the book.

CONTINUE TO BE AMAZING
LaTasha Nicole
Peace!

Acknowledgements

A thank you to each of you reading this, I hope this book is the spark that you need to ignite the change that you want to see.

Thank to those that have supported me through my many adventures and have taken this crazy ride with me.

Thank you to my late night study buddy, for staying up and helping me sort through my stuff. I appreciate your patience and I thank you for loving me.

To Mike, because of you I am a stronger me. For that I thank you.

To my uncles consider this your "rose" from 1991. Thanks for always having my back.

About the Author

LaTasha Nicole is a certified Small Business Development Coach, a passionate speaker, the founder of The Next 100 Project, co-author of The Entrepreneur Within You 3 and creator of the First Impressions Customer Service and Soft Skills Training Program.

Known as an innovative and creative business strategist, she has helped numerous women and small businesses expand their opportunities.

Connect with LaTasha Nicole
Twitter @itislatashanic

www.itislatashanicole.com

Notes

Notes

Notes

Notes

Notes

www.ingramcontent.com/pod-product-compliance
Lightning Source LLC
Chambersburg PA
CBHW060638100426
42744CB00008B/1676

I want to leave you with some of my favorite quotes. Hopefully they will leave an imprint on you as they have done for me.

"Change your thinking, change your choices, change your life."

"Intentional living is about knowing why it is that you do what do, and why you do not do the things that you do not do."

"Be inspired!"

"Live well, Love hard, Laugh often!"

"Success is personal."

"Think different!"

"I don't quit when I'm tired, I quit when I'm done."

"Anything is possible!"

Dream big, ladies! Go forth, and conquer the world!

You got this!
-LaTasha Nicole